PIGEONS

For Elizabeth

PIGEONS by Bernice Kohn Hunt
Copyright © 1973 by Bernice Kohn Hunt
Illustrations © 1973 by Bruce Waldman

Printed in the United States of America • 2

Prentice-Hall International, Inc., London
Prentice-Hall of Australia, Pty. Ltd., North Sydney
Prentice-Hall of Canada, Ltd., Toronto
Prentice-Hall of India Private Ltd., New Delhi
Prentice-Hall of Japan, Inc., Tokyo

Library of Congress Cataloging in Publication Data

Hunt, Bernice Kohn.
  Pigeons.

    SUMMARY: Briefly introduces the history and habits
of several varieties of pigeons.
    1. Pigeons—Juvenile literature.   [1. Pigeons]
I. Waldman, Bruce, illus. II. Title.
QL696.C6H86   598.6'5   72-13942
ISBN 0-13-676304-9

Prentice-Hall. Inc., Englewood Cliffs, New Jersey

PIGEONS

by Bernice Kohn Hunt

illustrated by Bruce Waldman

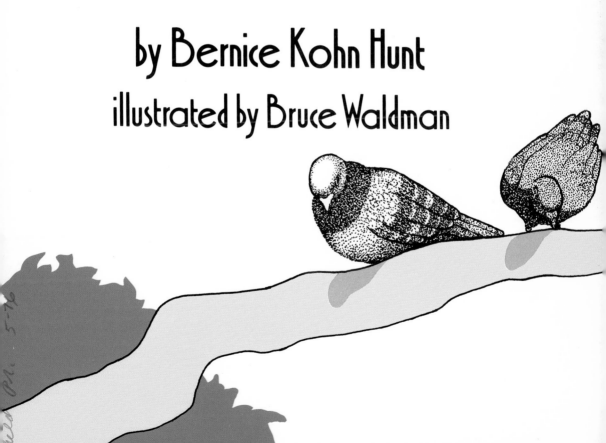

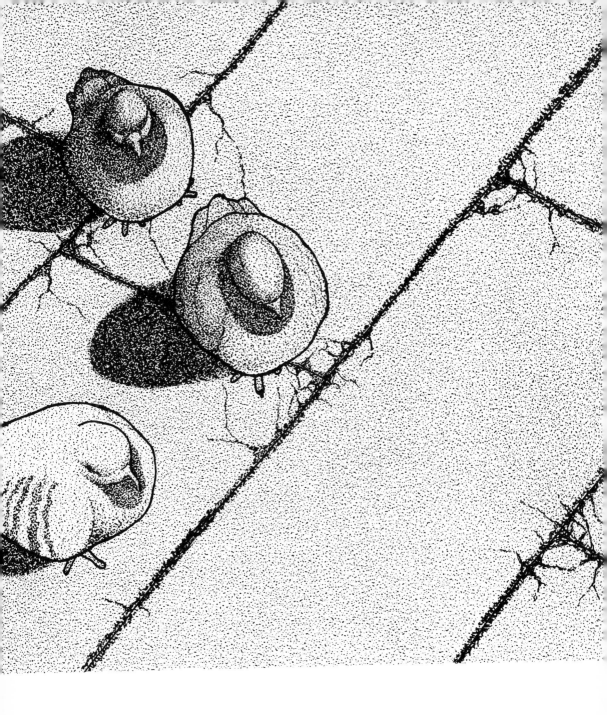

If you live in a city, you probably see pigeons every day. You can see them on your way to school early in the morning. Pigeons are up and about as soon as it begins to turn light.

Pigeons are fairly large doves, from 11 to 13 inches long. Males and females look about the same. They have fan-shaped tails and they bob their heads as they walk around on their short legs. Their call is a gentle coo-oo-oo.

U. S. **1903373**

Unlike most other birds, pigeons do not have to hold their heads back when they drink in order to let the liquid run down their throats. They take up water with their bills and swallow it, the way you drink with a straw.

The domestic pigeon is our common bird of city parks. It is even found on city streets if there are a few trees—or underfoot at crowded fairs and carnivals where peanuts or popcorn are often dropped.

Our pigeon is the rock dove, *Columba livia*. As a country bird, it made its home on rocky cliffs.

Now it seeks the man-made cliffs of ledges and sills on city buildings.

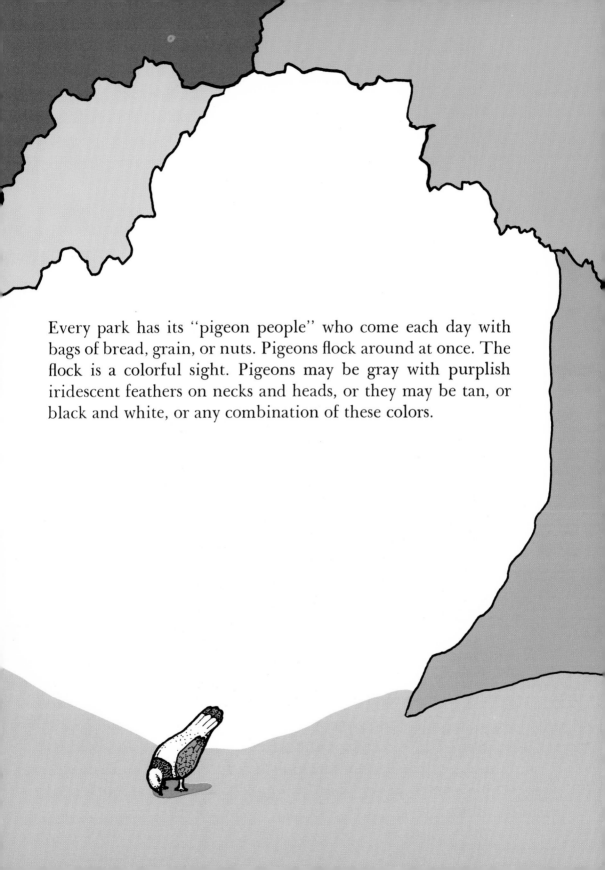

Every park has its "pigeon people" who come each day with bags of bread, grain, or nuts. Pigeons flock around at once. The flock is a colorful sight. Pigeons may be gray with purplish iridescent feathers on necks and heads, or they may be tan, or black and white, or any combination of these colors.

When pigeons mate, they usually select pigeons with the same coloring as themselves. They probably pick birds that look like their parents. A pair of pigeons stay together all during breeding time. Their nest is a messy affair; it is quite flat, barely turning up at the edge, and it is made of twigs, straw, or any suitable scraps. It seems carelessly thrown together and, in fact, it does sometimes fall apart or topple from its perch on a wall or branch.

The female lays two white eggs and sits on them for about 17 days. The father often takes a turn at keeping the eggs warm. After the naked young hatch, both mother and father feed them by regurgitating partly digested food into the babies' mouths. Within five weeks, the chicks are able to fly and take care of themselves.

Pigeons are hardy and can make their way in many kinds of places. They feed on seeds, grain, and many fruits and vegetables. On the outskirts of towns, they often peck at food in garbage dumps. They even find edible seeds and berries on beaches.

Pigeons have gotten along under different conditions for a long time. We know from old documents that the Egyptians raised pigeons 3000 years ago and that pigeon-keeping was a popular hobby in ancient Rome.

The Romans built beautiful rooftop pigeon coops. When conquering Roman soldiers overran much of Europe, some took their pigeons with them. In this way, the custom of pigeon-keeping reached Britain, and later, colonists brought it to the New World.

Although pigeon-raising is no longer as popular as it once was, we still see rooftop dovecotes here and there. Pigeons are easy to keep as pets. They can be bought in many pet stores. They learn to recognize their owners quickly and willingly go for a ride atop a head or shoulder.

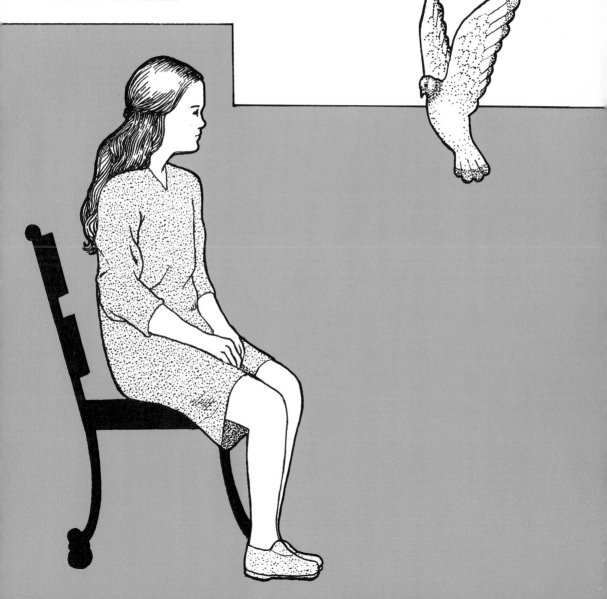

Blue-barred pouter

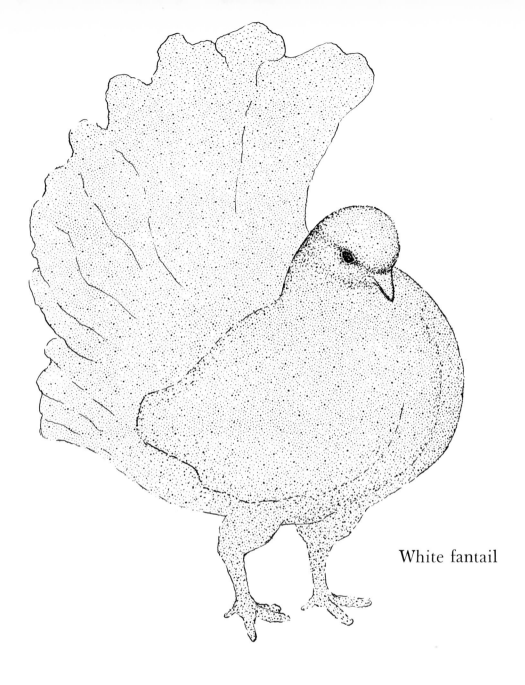

White fantail

Some people raise pigeons to exhibit in shows. They favor fan-
tails, frillbacks, trumpeters, or pouters.

Other people raise pigeons for racing. The homing pigeon is ideal for this exciting sport. Its training begins when the owner releases the very young bird a short distance from home. The pigeon always finds its way straight back to the coop, but no one knows just how. As the bird grows older and stronger, the distance from home is lengthened. By the time it is two or three years old, a pigeon can find its way back from as far away as 500 miles!

During wartime, homing pigeons have been used to carry messages. Their strong wings sped them high above the battlefields. No one could tell that there were secret messages in tiny tubes strapped to the birds' legs.

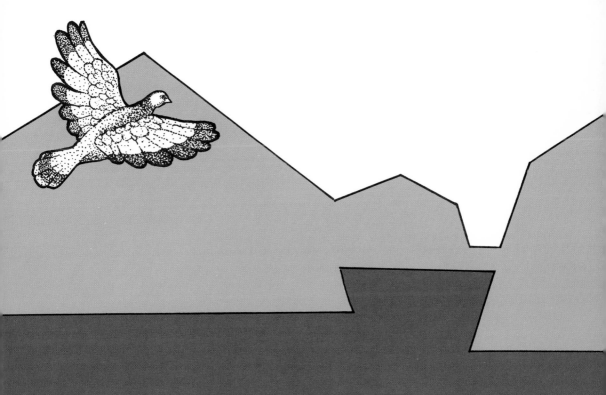

Mourning dove

The pigeons *we* see are not usually heros! They are plain city pigeons. When city people visit the country, they often think mourning doves are pigeons. Although they are closely related, mourning doves have pointed tails and a black spot behind each eye.

These birds did not spread
out to roost but crowded together in trees. They crowded
so closely that their weight
caused many branches to
break and crash to the
ground.

U. S. **1903373**

Passenger pigeon

Mourning doves look very much like the now extinct passenger
pigeon. During colonial times, this was our most common bird.

Passenger pigeons flew in flocks so large that they made the sky as dark as dusk for hours at a time. One report of a roosting flock tells us that it covered an area three miles wide and 40 miles long!

During the settling of the Midwest, hungry pioneers came to collect the pigeons wherever they flocked. They had only to shoot at a tree and hundreds of birds would fall down. Farmers used them for fresh food, salted them for the winter, or fed them to hogs. Many shot pigeons just for sport.

The careless killing was so great that our most common bird became more and more scarce. Finally, on the first day of September, 1914, the last known specimen died of old age in the Cincinnati Zoo. No passenger pigeon has ever been seen in this country since.

Fortunately, most people have learned that we must take care of our birds. If we do, our city pigeons will be with us for a long time to come.

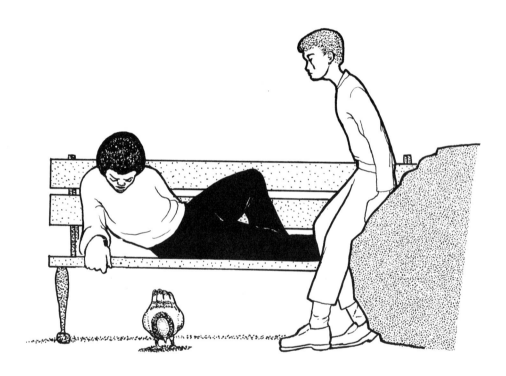